Shapes

Preschool/Kindergarten

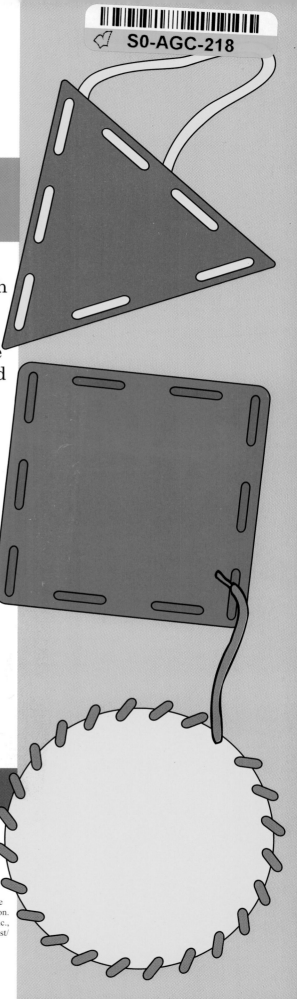

Save time and energy planning thematic units with this comprehensive resource. We've searched the 1990–1998 issues of **The MAILBOX®** and **Teacher's Helper®** magazines to find the best ideas for you to use when teaching a thematic unit about shapes. Included in this book are favorite units from the magazines, single ideas to extend a unit, and a variety of reproducible activities. Use these shapely activities to develop your own complete unit or simply to enhance your current lesson plans. You're sure to find everything you need for shaping student learning.

Project Manager:
Michele M. Stoffel Menzel

Editor:
Thad H. McLaurin

Cover Artist:
Kimberly Richard

www.themailbox.com

Table Of Contents

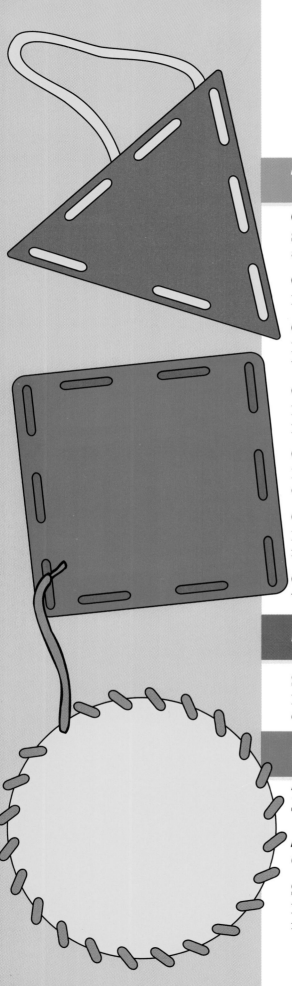

Thematic Units...

from The MAILBOX® magazine

Get In Shape

Get your little ones into shapes with this well-rounded unit about circles.

ideas by Carrie Lacher

Buried Treasure

Set sail for an adventure on the high seas of learning with this discovery lesson about circles. To prepare for a class treasure hunt, gather a collection of round objects such as container lids, toy rings and bracelets, large buttons, juice-can lids, and poker chips. On the day of the hunt, hide the objects in your sand table. Place a supply of pails and scoopers nearby. Collect magazine pictures in which circular objects can be seen. Mount the pictures on construction paper and laminate the papers or place them in plastic page protectors. Display the pictures near the sand table. Or locate a copy of *Round & Round & Round* by Tana Hoban (check your library). On or near your sand table, place a sign that reads "Discover a treasure of circles!"

Gather your crew together and weave a tale of shipwrecked pirates. Describe to them a treasure that was buried on a forgotten island. Lead youngsters on a voyage through your classroom; then "land" at the sand table. Read aloud the sign that challenges them to discover circles. Carefully examine and discuss the displayed pictures or the pictures in *Round & Round & Round*. Then encourage them to dig into the sand to get a real feel for circles.

Circles All Around

Seat youngsters in a circle and ask them to brainstorm a list of items that are round. Write their suggestions on a large, bulletin-board-paper circle. As youngsters brainstorm, lead them to name food items that can be circular in shape such as snack crackers, LifeSavers®, Cheerios®, pancakes, and orange or banana slices. Designate a day to be "Circle Day." Send a note home with each child asking him to bring a requested food item to school on that day. When the items arrive at school, arrange them on a round table that is covered with a round tablecloth. Provide each child with a paper plate; then encourage him to select the round items of his choice for snacking. The good-health reminder of the day? Don't forget to eat your circles!

Snacktime Shape-Up

Use these placemats at snacktime to help little ones define their space and to build shape-recognition skills. Personalize a large, white, construction-paper circle for each child. Provide youngsters with a supply of dot stickers and sponge-tipped dot markers for decorating the circles. Or make your own circular stamps by cutting circles from foam insoles. Mount the fabric side of each foam circle onto a sanded wood scrap. Encourage each child to press the stamps onto inkpads, then onto her paper circle.

When each child has decorated her placemat, ask her to describe her work. Write her comments on her mat; then laminate it or cover it with Con-Tact® covering to protect it from spills and crumbs. Read aloud the comments on a different placemat each day during snacktime.

Discover A Treasure Of Circles!

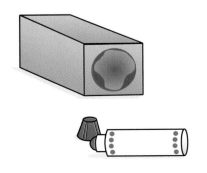

These circles are bubbles. They are flying.

Tabitha

With Circles

It's Circle Time!

Here's a riddle for your little ones. What do circles like best about preschool? Circle time—of course! Incorporate this movement activity into your group time and youngsters will soon be going around in circles. Using chalk draw a large circle on the floor of your group area; then cover the chalk outline with colorful tape. Invite the children to stand on the tape. Get those math muscles moving with this shapely song sung to the tune of "If You're Happy And You Know It." Create new verses by changing the movement from *tiptoe slowly* to *stomp your feet, slide sideways, hippity hop,* and more! Go ahead...act silly on the circle and go round!

A circle is a shape that goes round.
A circle is a shape that goes round.
A circle is a shape that goes round and
    round and round.
A circle is a shape that goes round.

[Tiptoe slowly] on the circle and go round.
[Tiptoe slowly] on the circle and go round.
[Tiptoe slowly] on the circle and go round
    and round and round.
[Tiptoe slowly] on the circle and go round.

Circle Prints

Get ready for squeals of delight when youngsters make this hands-on art project. Tape a large piece of bubble wrap (bubble side up) onto a flat surface. Invite a child to spread washable paint over the slippery, bumpy wrap. (Provide foam brushes for the sensorially squeamish.) Then have him quickly wash and dry his hands before pressing a large, construction-paper circle onto the wrap. Have him peel off the paper to reveal a collection of printed circles. When the prints are dry, provide magnifiers and display the prints where your circle explorers can examine up close the variations in the multitude of circles.

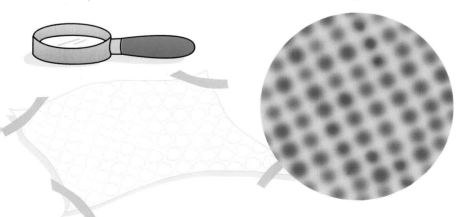

Going In Search Of Circles

Now that youngsters have experienced circles in a variety of ways indoors, it's time to take your circle search to the streets. Lead youngsters on a circle walk around your school, keeping a list as the students observe circles along the way.

Include families in on the fun by sending home a circular note suggesting that they conduct their own circle hunt.

Dear Parent, Go on a circle hunt! Help your child learn about circles by looking for circles at home.

Well-Rounded Reading

Circles, Triangles, And Squares
Written & Photographed by
Tana Hoban
(Check your library.)

Ten Black Dots
Written & Illustrated by
Donald Crews
Published by Mulberry Books

Wheel Away!
Written by Dayle Ann Dodds
Illustrated by Thacher Hurd
(Check your library.)

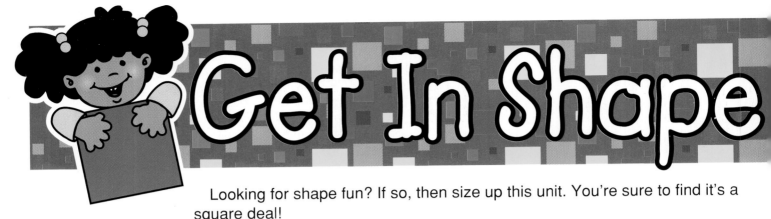

Get In Shape

Looking for shape fun? If so, then size up this unit. You're sure to find it's a square deal!

ideas contributed by Linda Rice Ludlow

Square Safari

In the jungle of your room are squares waiting to be discovered! To help your little ones spy squares, prepare "binocu-squares." To make a pair, cut off the end flaps from a margarine box. Draw a vertical line through the center of the back of the box and cut. Press the box flat so that the printed side is facing down. Fold one end of the box onto itself to meet the first crease; then fold again twice. Fold the opposite end in the same manner. Release; then refold each side to create rectangular tubes. Fold both tubes once again so that the sides touch in the center. Secure the tubes with tape. If desired, cover the completed pair of "binocu-squares" with paper.

Have each child look through a pair of the "binocu-squares" in search of unsuspecting squares around your room. At snacktime hide individual bags of square-shaped snacks such as crackers or sandwich quarters; then have youngsters search for the bags around the room. Everywhere, there's a square!

Celebrity Square

Make a square puppet to add personality to your focus on squares. Since your puppet is sure to be a celebrity, assist each child in making a square puppet of his own. To make a puppet, cut a construction-paper rectangle that measures exactly twice as long as it is wide. Fold the rectangle in half; then glue only the sides together. Encourage each child to use small paper squares and markers as desired to add facial features to his square. Teach youngsters the following song and encourage them to help their square puppets sing along!

Ode To A Square

(sung to the tune of "Clementine")

I have four sides
All the same size,
And my shape is called a square.
I can be so very useful,
And I'm seen 'most everywhere!

With Squares

The Mystery Of The Missing Square

Youngsters are sure to enjoy this shaped-up version of the game Doggy, Doggy, Who's Got Your Bone? To play, seat youngsters in a group. Ask a volunteer to sit in a chair with his back facing the group. Place a square cutout beneath the chair. Then silently motion for a child in the group to take the square, return to the group, and hide the square behind him. As a group chant, "[Child's name], [child's name], in the chair. Somebody came and took your square." The child in the chair then makes as many as four guesses (one for each side of the square) as to who took the square. Whether or not he guesses correctly, praise him for his effort and invite him to trade places with the child holding the square.

Gift-Wrapped Squares

Snacktime is all wrapped up with this special snack. Give each child a graham-cracker square to "wrap" by spreading it with frosting. If desired, have her decorate her package by adding candy sprinkles. To top the package with a bow, have her place a whole gumdrop on the center of the cracker, and then arrange four gumdrop halves around the whole gumdrop. This is one gift-wrapped package children won't have to wait to enjoy!

Squarely Centered

Get your blocks center all squared away with these suggestions. Remove all but the cube-shaped squares from your blocks center. Supplement the center with other cube-shaped items such as gift-wrapped boxes, square nesting cups, and plastic containers with lids. As each child builds, ask him to find the square sides of the blocks, boxes, containers, and lids in his structure.

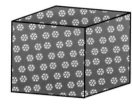 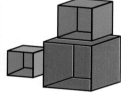

Be A Square!

You won't have to go on a square hunt to find youngsters who are willing to participate in this group activity. Divide your class into groups of four children each. Ask each child in a group to stand with her arms out; then show the children how to stand beside and in front of each other to form a group square. Then teach youngsters this shapely song.

We're A Square

(sung to the tune of "London Bridge")

Our four sides are just the same.
Just the same. Just the same.
Our four sides are just the same.
We're a square.

Get In Shape

Teach youngsters about triangles with these fun activities that get right to the point.

ideas by Pamela Kay Priest

Triangle Town

Where's the best place to learn about triangles? Triangle Town, of course! In an open area of your room, establish the boundaries of Triangle Town by using colored tape to tape the outline of a large triangle onto the floor. Randomly tape smaller triangles inside the large triangle to create a maze of roads. Provide youngsters with various colors of construction-paper triangles, markers, glue, and cardboard tubes. Encourage them to create triangle trees and signs for Triangle Town. Supply triangular-shaped blocks and small cars for youngsters to play with while visiting the town.

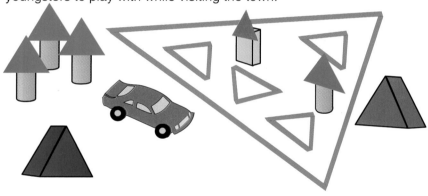

Let's Bowl!

Youngsters will shape up their triceps as they set up triangles in this easy-to-make game of bowling. Locate an area suitable for bowling, such as a sidewalk, a hall, or an open area of your classroom. Set up ten cardboard tubes to form a triangle. Mark around the triangular tube arrangement with chalk. If the bowling lane will be indoors, tape over the chalk to indicate the area for the arrangement of the bowling tubes. If desired, also mark the spot where each tube should be placed to form the bowling arrangement. To play, a child rolls a soft ball toward the set-up tubes as if bowling. Encourage each child to count the tubes in the triangle arrangement when preparing for the next set. Let's go for three strikes in a row!

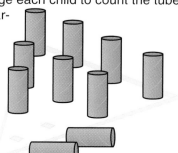

Musical Triangles

Accompany your triangle activities with the instrument of the day—the triangle. To make a triangle for each child, bend the hook of a hanger into a loop; then thread a four-inch length of yarn through the loop and tie it. Demonstrate how to hold the triangle by the yarn while tapping it lightly with a spoon. Give each child a triangle and spoon to play as children sing this triangle tune. Model how to keep a steady beat by tapping on the instrument. At the end of the song, tap each corner or side of the triangle as you sing, "One, two, three!"

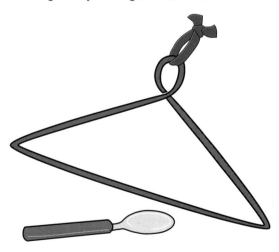

This Is A Triangle

(sung to the tune of "Row, Row, Row Your Boat")

This is a triangle.
Look and you will see.
It has three corners and three sides.
Count them. One, two, three!

With Triangles

Talking Turkey

This crafty turkey is a totally triangular dude! To make a turkey, each child will need a large, brown construction-paper triangle; a small, brown triangle; a supply of colorful construction-paper squares (including orange and red); glue; markers; and scissors. Glue the small, brown triangle to the larger triangle to represent the turkey's head and body. Cut the various colors of squares in half diagonally; then glue the resulting triangles to the back of the turkey's body in order to feather him. Cut an orange square in half diagonally; then glue each triangle to the base of the turkey to resemble legs. Color eyes; then glue small orange and red triangles to the tip of the turkey's head to create a beak and a wattle. So that the turkeys will be unique, provide each child with colored glue for embellishing the feathers of his turkey.

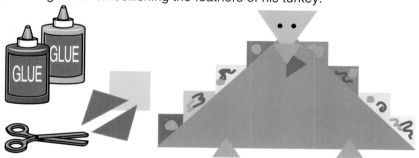

Two's Company, Three's A...Triangle!

Capture memories of your little ones getting into shape by creating this unique photo album. Place a large sheet of bulletin-board paper on the floor. Invite groups of three children at a time to lie on the paper and together form a triangle with their whole bodies, legs, arms, or fingers. Encourage each team to be creative. Take a picture of each group's pose. Glue each developed picture to a triangular-shaped piece of construction paper; then write the pictured students' names on the page. To make a photo album, title a cover "Triangles Of Friends"; then bind the pages together. Or display four, nine, or sixteen of the triangular-shaped pages together to form a giant triangle.

Jay, Brice, Justin

Triangle Problem Solving

The point of this center is to get youngsters' hands on triangles while developing their problem-solving skills as well. Store about 40 craft sticks in a container. As a group of children visits the center, demonstrate how to make a triangle using three sticks. Ask the children to help you count the sides and the corners of the triangle. Challenge the group to make as many triangles as they can or to make one giant triangle with the craft sticks. Encourage partners to make triangles with common sides. Before you know it, your little ones will have turned a corner on creative thinking.

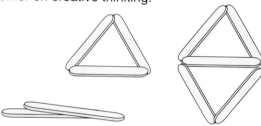

Eating To Stay In Shape

Eating to stay in shape is easy when the treats are triangles as well! Cut slices of bread, square sandwich meat, and cheese slices into triangles. If desired also provide condiments such as mayonnaise and mustard. Allow each child to make his own sandwich. On the side serve triangular-shaped chips and triangles cut from fruit rolls for dessert. Don't forget to provide square napkins folded into triangles. Why count calories when you can count corners? Shapely eating is as easy as one, two, three!

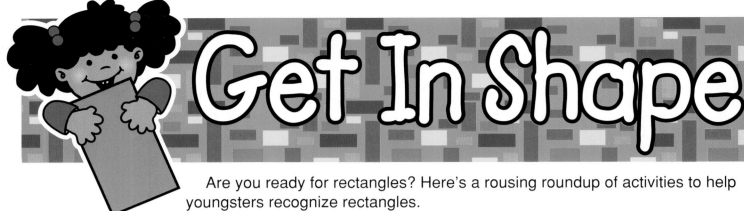

Get In Shape

Are you ready for rectangles? Here's a rousing roundup of activities to help youngsters recognize rectangles.

by Angie Kutzer

Recognizing Rectangles

Gather a collection of empty food boxes with front panels that are rectangular in shape. Cut off the front panels; then show them to students during a group time. Ask volunteers to select panels and point out the long and short sides. Then encourage children to look for rectangular-shaped food boxes at home. Send a note to parents requesting that empty food boxes be sent to class. Set aside a few different-sized boxes for "Panel Printing" (below); then cut the front panels from the remaining boxes for use with the following activities.

Tall Or Short: Challenge volunteers to arrange the collection of rectangles so that they're all "standing tall"—so that the long sides are vertical—or "lying long"—so that the long sides are horizontal.

Rectangle Reading: To help little ones begin to recognize environmental print, display labels in a collage on a bulletin board or wall. Provide a pointer and encourage little ones to read the names of the foods or brands.

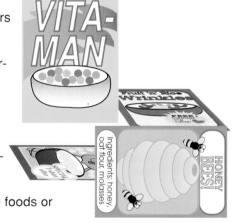

Panel Printing: Put your collection of uncut, empty food boxes in the art center. Pour several different colors of paint into separate shallow trays. Have a child dip the panel of a box into a tray. Then have him press the box onto a large sheet of construction paper. Encourage him to use different sizes of boxes and different colors to make his rectangular relic.

"Panel Printing" by Diana Byrne—Pre-K Harleysville, PA

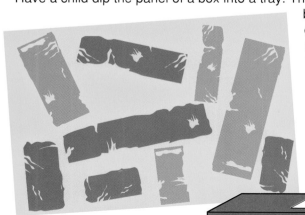

Romp And Rollick Round The Rectangle

Add a little rhythm and rhyme to your rectangle study. Using colored tape, make a large rectangle outline on your classroom floor. If desired, use one color of tape for the long sides and a different color for the short sides. Give each child a pair of building blocks or a set of sand blocks. Play excerpts from various slow and fast recordings. Encourage students to keep the beat with the blocks and their feet as they travel around the tape shape. For added fun, have them "freeze" every time the music stops. Look, we're doing the "rec-tango"!

Diana Byrne—Pre-K

Postcard Puzzlers

Get children's visual-discrimination and critical-thinking skills in shape with these rectangular puzzles. Gather an assortment of postcards. Cut each card into two or three pieces to make a postcard puzzle. Store each puzzle in a rectangular envelope. Or, for an added challenge, store the pieces to several cards in one envelope. Rectangles and postcards are a perfect fit!

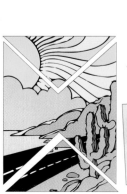

With Rectangles

Rectangle Rodeo

Head out to the Rectangle Ranch to let your little broncobusters show-case their talents. Students will exercise their fine-motor skills and hand/eye coordination when making these rectangular horses *and* when bringing them back into the corral.

To make a horse, cut two 3" x 1 1/2" and one 6" x 3" white, black, brown, or tan rectangles from construction paper. Glue the rectangles together as shown. Cut lengths of yarn; then glue them to the horse to create a mane and tail. Glue one wiggle eye to each side of the horse's head. When the glue is dry, attach clothespins to the bottom of the rectangular body to represent the horse's legs. Personalize the horse; then slide a paper clip onto the horse's back.

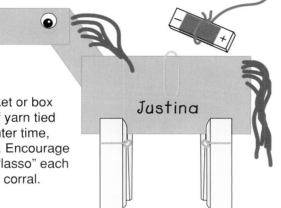

Justina

Place the horses in a basket or box (corral) along with a length of yarn tied around a magnet. During center time, stand the horses on the floor. Encourage a child to use the magnet to "lasso" each horse and put it back into the corral. Yippee-ki-yay!

Riddles On Rectangles

Collect a variety of objects that have a rectangular shape. (Refer to the following riddles for suggestions.) For each item, tell a riddle to help youngsters guess the identity of the object. Display the whole collection of items at all times. Once children are familiar with the objects, hide them in a box or bag. Pull out one at a time as guessed. What has two long and two short sides? A rectangle!

What Am I?

1. I am a rectangle. I can stand up or be hung on a wall. I decorate the edges of photographs. What am I? *(picture frame)*

2. I am a rectangle. I have lots of illustrations and words. I tell a story. What am I? *(book)*

3. I am a rectangle. I am sturdy and strong. The third little pig used me to build his house. What am I? *(brick)*

4. I am a rectangle—that is, until you chew me. I come in lots of different flavors. You can buy me in a little or big package. What am I? *(stick of gum)*

The Long And Short Of It

Help little ones differentiate between *squares* and *rectangles* with this catchy song. Hold up a rectangle and a square while singing the first verse, then just the rectangle during the second verse. Encourage the children to clap while singing the phrase "It's a rectangle," each time.

It's A Rectangle
(sung to the tune of "B-I-N-G-O")

There is a shape that has four sides,
But it is not a square....No!
It's a rectangle;
It's a rectangle;
It's a rectangle;
It is not like a square....No!

Two sides are long; two sides are short.
They all are not the same....No!
It's a rectangle;
It's a rectangle;
It's a rectangle;
The sides are not the same....No!

Get In Shape

Dazzle your youngsters as you use these sparkling activities to introduce the diamond shape.

ideas by Suzanne Moore

Presto "Change-o"

Amaze your little ones by introducing the diamond shape in this magical way. To prepare, spread glue onto the dull side of an 8" x 10" piece of foil. Press the foil onto a 9" x 12" piece of black construction paper. (Be sure the foil is completely attached to the paper so it does not separate during your magic act.) When the glue is dry, fold the paper in half so that the foil is inside. Using a pencil, lightly draw a five-inch-tall triangle on the black paper so that the base of the triangle is on the fold.

During a group time, keep the paper folded as you show your audience both sides. Review the attributes of a triangle as you dramatically cut it out of the paper. Holding the cutout at the top point, show the shape to the class. Then say the magic words, "Abracadabra, zim zam zimond. Turn this triangle into a diamond!" Flip the triangle open to reveal the diamond shape. If desired, follow up your trick by having students make their own magic diamonds in a similar manner.

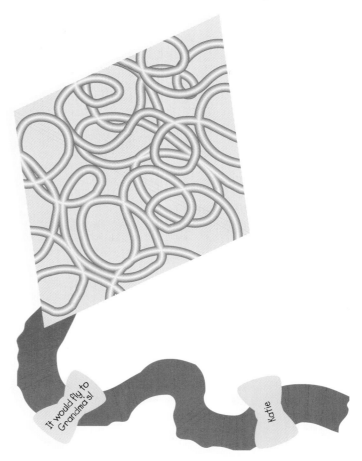

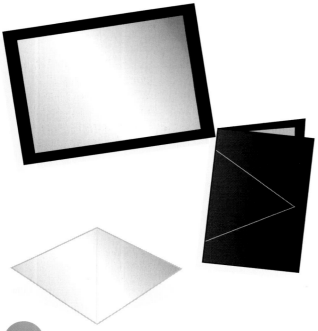

Let's Go Fly A Kite

Youngsters will be flying high—and getting a real feel for diamonds—when they make these fingerpainted kites. For each child, cut a used file folder into a diamond shape. Also cut two bow shapes from construction paper, and a length of crepe-paper streamer. Have the child place his shape on a cookie sheet or lunch tray; then provide him with various colors of fingerpaint. As he paints, help him describe the attributes of the diamond. Ask the child to set his kite aside to dry and to wash his hands. On one bow, write his description of where his kite would fly. Write his name on the second bow. Tape the bows to the streamer; then tape the streamer to the back of the kite. Suspend the kites from your ceiling. Look! Diamonds in the sky!

With Diamonds

Diamond Necklaces

These necklaces will polish off youngsters' abilities to recognize the diamond shape. For each child, cut a 5" x 3" diamond from tagboard, a 5" square from aluminum foil, and a 24" length of thick, glittery yarn. To make a necklace, wrap the foil around the shape. Punch a hole near the top of the shape; then thread the yarn through the hole. Tie the yarn at the top of the shape (so that it will lie flat when worn) and at the yarn ends. If desired, glue rhinestones to each of the four corners of the diamond. Diamond days are here again!

A Crown Of Diamonds

Your little kings and queens will feel like royalty when wearing these diamond-decorated crowns. Cut several tagboard diamond shapes and foil squares (as described in "Diamond Necklaces") for each child. Have each child cover each of her shapes with foil, then glue on craft jewels. Staple her decorated diamonds onto a sturdy sentence strip; then staple the ends of the strip so the crown fits on the child's head. Look! It's the duke and duchess of diamonds!

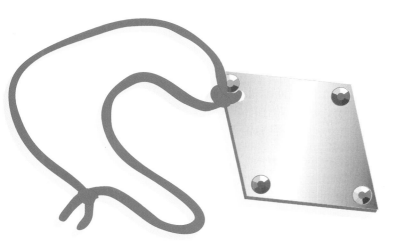

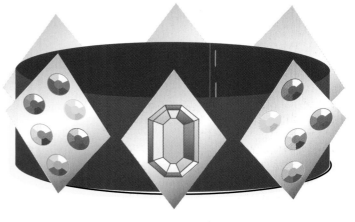

One Big Diamond

Follow up your kite craft (see "Let's Go Fly A Kite") by chanting this poem. If desired, draw a kite on a chalkboard. As you recite the poem, erase the tail of the kite to reveal a diamond.

> One big diamond high in flight.
> A diamond's shaped just like a kite.
> Take away the tail, and what do I see?
> A diamond looking back at me!

Home Run!

This movement idea is sure to be a hit! If your school has a baseball field, take youngsters out for a run around the giant diamond shape. Or arrange four game cones, game base markers, or placemats in an open area of your playground to indicate the four corners of a diamond. Have the class follow you as you run to each of the four corners of the diamond shape. Now that's a home run of an idea!

Diamond Jubilee

Diamonds are fun to wear but even more fun to eat! Invite your necklace- and crown-clad youngsters to visit a cooking center to prepare these delicious diamonds. To make one, cut a piece of bread into a diamond shape; then spread butter and jam onto the bread. Diamond desserts fit for royalty!

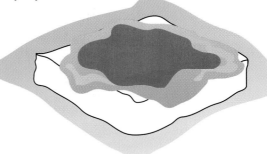

Get In Shape

Here it is! Our last set of exercises created to get your preschoolers into great shape! Use these activities to round out youngsters' knowledge of that oh-so-original oval.

ideas contributed by Barbara Meyers and Angie Kutzer

Looking For Ovals

Enlist the help of Little Oval to search for ovals in the classroom. To make the costume, cut a slit three-fourths of the way down both narrow sides of a paper grocery bag. Cut out an oval shape from tagboard, large enough to cover one of the wider sides of the bag; then glue it to the bag. Ask a child to put on the costume so that you can mark where to cut a smaller oval about the size of a child's face. Then cut the oval through both the bag and the larger oval. Label the costume "Little Oval."

Begin your oval unit by reading aloud *The Shape Of Things* by Dayle Ann Dodds (Candlewick Press). After reading, turn back to the page that focuses on ovals. Introduce the shape's name again and have youngsters trace imaginary ovals in the air. Invite a volunteer to put on the costume and become Little Oval. While the group quietly sings the following song, send him on a search to find an oval-shaped object in the classroom. Once the song ends, have Little Oval share his find.

Look What I Found!
(sung to the tune of "Five Little Ducks")

Oval shape went out one day
To find more oval shapes to play.
Oval shape looked all around,
Then with a smile said, "Look what I found!"

Little Oval

Optical Ovals

What can you do with potatoes, paint, and paper? Make oodles of oval prints! To get ready for the printing, slice several potatoes in half lengthwise; then fill several pie pans with different colors of tempera paint. Look again at the printed shapes in *The Shape Of Things*. Invite each student to dip a potato half into the paint and print several oval shapes onto a large sheet of art paper. When the paint is dry, encourage her to use markers and precut construction-paper shapes to turn her oval into a masterpiece. Display these creations along with the title "Can You Find The Ovals?" for others to ogle over.

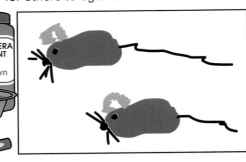

Oval Munchies

Your little ones are sure to be in great shape after making and munching on these "oval-wiches" at the cooking center. To make one, use an oval-shaped cookie cutter to cut an oval from two slices of bread and one slice of processed cheese. Place one oval of bread on an oval-shaped plate or a napkin cut into an oval shape; then add the oval of cheese. Squirt an oval of mustard or mayonnaise on top of the cheese before topping the sandwich with the second oval of bread. Lean to the left; lean to the right. Pick up your "oval-wich"; then take a bite!

With Ovals

The Oval Song

Use colored tape to make a large oval shape on the floor; then invite your little ones to hop, skip, march, and otherwise move around the tape while singing this catchy oval song.

I'm An Oval

(sung to the tune of "I'm A Little Teapot")

I'm an oval made with a curved line.
I think my egg shape looks mighty
   fine.
Eggs, potatoes, spoons, and race-
   tracks, too:
All have oval shapes just for you!

Get A Feel For It

Little fingers will do the walking with this tactile activity. Insert a variety of plastic or cardboard geometric shapes into a bag or box. (Make sure that there are more ovals than other shapes.) Challenge each child to reach into the bag and pull out an oval. Feeling for ovals is fun!

Stretch And Shape, Stretch And Shape

Cooperation is the key to this shapely exercise. To prepare, sew together the ends of a four-yard length of one-inch-wide elastic. Ask each child in a small group to hold onto the loop and work together to make an elastic oval shape. As a challenge, have the group stretch the loop into previously studied shapes, then back into an oval. What a workout!

Jelly-Bean Jamboree

End your shape training session with the best oval shapes of all—Jelly Belly® jelly beans! Fill a clear container with an assortment of the gourmet jelly beans. Seat your youngsters in an oval; then pass the container around the oval for each child to observe. List volunteers' descriptions about what they see. When the container returns to you, dispense a few jelly beans to each child. Encourage the students to touch, taste, and talk about the samples as you add to the descriptive list. (Be sure to use close supervision since jelly beans may be a choking hazard.) For added fun, request that your little ones try to guess the flavors of their jelly beans. Explain to your students that the candy company would like new jelly-bean designs and flavors. Give each child an oval-shaped paper platter, and invite him to use his choice of colorful paints and painting sponges to create his own jelly bean. As each child describes his jelly bean and names its flavor, ask the group to name the jelly bean's shape. Ovals, ovals, ovals!

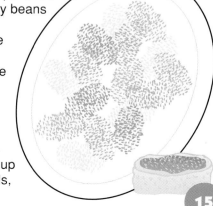

GEOMETRIC GYM

When it's time to get into shapes, visit this gym for a thorough workout with circles, squares, rectangles, and triangles.

by Lucia Kemp Henry

Working Out With What's Available

Use this rhyming riddle to introduce your youngsters to the shapes around them. Before sharing the rhyme with your students, use a photocopier to enlarge the picture cards on page 20. Then color and cut apart the cards along the grid lines. If desired, prepare these illustrated cards for flannelboard use. When sharing the rhyme with students, have youngsters scan the picture cards and locate an illustration to match each clue given in lines 5 through 20.

Shapes

Shapes can help us every day.
We use shapes for work and play.
Square, circle, rectangle—triangle too!
Look and find the shapes—all around you.

A square is a place to lay your head.   (a pillow)
A square is a scarf that's colored red.   (a bandana)
Squares let the sun in, bright as can be.   (a window)
Squares on the floor make patterns you see.   (tiles)

A triangle's a sign for cars in the street.   (a yield sign)
A triangle's a slice of something to eat.   (a pizza slice)
Triangles are hats for party fun.   (a party hat)
Camp in a triangle when the day is done.   (a tent)

A circle can roll along the ground.   (a tire)
A circle can bounce up and down.   (a ball)
A circle is a fresh, tasty pie.   (a pie)
A circle is something in the sky.   (the sun)

A rectangle is a frame for something pretty.   (a picture frame)
A rectangle holds shoes for country or city.   (a shoebox)
Rectangles are places for fish to stay.   (an aquarium)
You can play football on a rectangle today.   (a football field)

—by Lucia Kemp Henry

Flip-The-Shapes Booklet

As a follow-up activity to the poem above, help your youngsters complete these small flip booklets. Reproduce the flip booklet cover and booklet pages (on pages 20–24) in classroom quantities. Using a paper cutter, cut along the bold outlines; then give each student a copy of each booklet page, the front cover, and a plain back cover (7 1/4" x 4 3/4"). Have each student color the book's components as he desires. Then have each child cut along the dotted lines and stack the four half-pages with the labeled shapes in one pile and the 12 half-pages with the picture shapes in another pile. Provide assistance as each child staples his two sets of booklet half-pages (as shown) between the covers of his booklet. Encourage youngsters to flip the pages to find ones with corresponding shapes.

TRDavidson

Exercise Your Brain

Designate a table for the display of geometrically shaped objects. Cover the tabletop with bulletin-board paper; then have students sponge-print circles, triangles, squares, and rectangles all over the paper. Ask students to bring in objects that are similar in shape to any of the sponge-printed shapes. As objects begin to collect on the table, give students opportunities to manipulate and name the shapes before sorting them into groups by shape.

Which One Is Missing?

Use the items collected in "Exercise Your Brain" as supplies for this game. Arrange some objects in a line on a small table. After showing the group of objects to your students, ask youngsters to close their eyes while you remove one of the items. When students open their eyes, ask them to determine which item is missing. Encourage students to use both the name and the shape of the object when specifying what's missing.

Secret Shapes

Play this question-and-answer game with the table full of objects collected in "Exercise Your Brain." Ask a few youngsters to stand at the shape table. Decide secretly on an object to be the focus of the first round of play. Have the youngsters at the table try to determine the object you have selected by asking a series of questions that can be answered with yes or no responses. Encourage students to begin with questions that will help them pinpoint the basic shape of the object you've selected. They might ask, for example, "Is the secret shape a circle [triangle, square, rectangle]?" As objects are eliminated by your responses, have students remove them from the table. Encourage students to continue by asking questions related to color, size, and purpose until only one object—the one you originally selected—remains on the table. Continue the game by replacing all the items on the table and secretly selecting (or having a child secretly select) an item to be the object for the next series of questions.

I found a magic triangle. It was able to change itself into anything like gold, or peppermint, or plastic. The magic shape said, "Take me with you." So I did. I used the shape to play music during free time and to play catch on the playground.

Getting Into Shapes—Like Magic!

Spark imagination and creative thinking with "magical" shapes. To prepare for this activity, cut large, colorful sheets of paper into oversize circles, squares, triangles, and rectangles. Set the stage for this activity by asking each student to choose a shape cutout and to pretend that it is magical. Then have each child, in turn, dictate completions for the following incomplete thoughts: "I found a magic…," "It was…," "The magic shape said,…," and "I used the shape to…." Using a colorful marker or metallic pen, write each student's dictation on his shape cutout.

I found a magic circle. It was able to grant wishes. The magic circle said, "You can have three wishes." I used the shape to wish for a new baseball hat, a trip to the amusement park, and a puppy.

The Creative Approach To Shaping Up

After your students have completed their stories about the magical shapes described in "Getting Into Shapes—Like Magic," give them an opportunity to make collages to display with the stories. To make a corresponding collage, start with a shape cutout to match the one bearing the story and glue it to art paper. Then use paint and a sponge of the same shape to sponge-print the paper and the shape. Glue on small gift-wrap cutouts to match the large shape. Use glitter and shape stickers to add the finishing touches to the shape collages. Display each student's collage with his dictated story from "Getting Into Shapes—Like Magic!" (page 17).

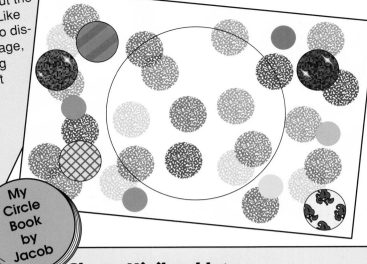

My Circle Book by Jacob

Shape Minibooklets

After you introduce a shape, wouldn't it be nice to send each youngster home with a small shape booklet? On colorful paper, duplicate multiple copies of shape designs for minibooklets. Have parent volunteers assist you by cutting out each copy of the shapes and stapling them into booklets. After you have introduced a shape, present each student with a copy of the corresponding shape minibooklet, and have him personalize its cover. To fill each page, have each student draw, glue on, or sponge-print an object shaped similarly to the booklet. If desired, students may write, copy, or dictate a label for each page, before taking the minibooklets home to share with their families.

Muscle Vests

Prepare brown paper grocery bags in advance for this activity. You'll need a bag for each child. Cut head and arm holes from each bag, and cut a slit up one side of the bag to create the basic vest shape. Provide paint and sponges that have been cut into circles, triangles, rectangles, and squares. Ask students to use these supplies to decorate the fronts and backs of their paper vests. If desired, have each child color, cut out, and glue on matching shape button cutouts. Wearing these "shapely" vests, students can march around the room singing a shape song like the one that follows.

Shaping Up To Music

Cooperation is important as youngsters strengthen their shape-recognition skills using this activity. Make a giant, imitation rubber band from 1/2-inch-wide elastic sewn into a loop. As you sing each verse of the shape song below, have several students stand within the confines of the giant rubber band to create a likeness of the featured shape.

ice-cream cone

Shapes

(Each verse of this song is sung to the tune of "London Bridge Is Falling Down.")

Two sides long and two sides short.
Two sides short. Two sides short.
Two sides long and two sides short.
We're a rectangle!

We're as round as we can be.
We can be. We can be.
We're as round as we can be.
We're a circle.

We've got three corners and three sides.
See our sides, with your eyes.
We've got three corners and three sides.
We're a triangle.

Our four sides are just the same.
Just the same. Just the same.
Our four sides are just the same.
We're a square.

—by Shelley Rubin

Shelley Rubin—Preschool, St. Andrew Preschool, Lynchburg, VA

"Martin-izing" Shapes

Red circle, red circle, What do you see?

If your students love Bill Martin, Jr's *Brown Bear, Brown Bear, What Do You See?*— and who doesn't?—they'll love this shape spin-off. Read aloud *Brown Bear, Brown Bear, What Do You See?*, and tell students that they will be making a similar book that contains shapes instead of animals. For the first page of the book, write, "Red circle, red circle, What do you see?" near the bottom of a sheet of paper. Program the second page of the book with something like, "I see a green rectangle looking at me." "Green rectangle, green rectangle, What do you see?" Continue programming any number of pages in a similar manner. When the pages have been programmed, pass each student a page and help him read the words. Then have him choose a shape from a collection you have provided or cut out and color one of his own and glue it to the page. Provide a final page that has a class photo and the words, "I see some boys and girls looking at me." Assemble and bind the booklet, and place it where youngsters can read it at their leisure.

Nina Tabanian—Gr. K, St. Rita School, Dallas, TX

Spotlighting Shapes

Here's a game that encourages shaping up! In preparation for the game, tape cutouts of basic shapes around your classroom. Put some on the walls, some on the doors, some on the floor, and even some on the ceiling. Then darken the room somewhat and give a flashlight to a child. Have him shine the light on a shape and identify the shape. Then have him shine the flashlight beam on shapes that match the one he originally identified. After a while, have the student pass the flashlight to another student, and repeat the process until each child has had a turn. Vary the routine, if desired, by calling out the names of shapes one after another as the student holding the flashlight illuminates a shape to match each one you named.

Jeannie Ryan—Gr. K, Provident Heights, Waco, TX

Breakfast For Champions

When you're really into shapes, you'll have something to celebrate. So consider culminating this unit with a breakfast featuring fruit pizza. For the party, have students spread strawberry-flavored cream cheese on a toasted piece of bread. Top with pineapple chunks, orange wedges, and sliced stawberries, grapes, and kiwi. As they chow down, encourage youngsters to comment on the shapes that they are eating.

Books To Really Help Youngsters Shape Up

Brown Rabbit's Shape Book
Written & Illustrated by Alan Baker
Published by Kingfisher Books

Afro-Bets®: Book Of Shapes
Written by Margery W. Brown & Illustrated by Culverson Blair
Published by Just Us Books

My Very First Book Of Shapes
Written & Illustrated by Eric Carle
(Check your library.)

The Wing On A Flea: A Book About Shapes
Written & Illustrated by Ed Emberley
(Check your library.)

Fire Engine Shapes
Written & Photographed by Bruce McMillan
(Check your library.)

Shapes, Shapes, Shapes
Written & Photographed by Tana Hoban
Published by Greenwillow Books

Circles, Triangles, And Squares
Written & Photographed by Tana Hoban
(Cneck your library.)

The Shape Of Me And Other Stuff
Written & Illustrated by Dr. Seuss
Published by Random House, Inc.

Picture Cards

Use with "Working Out With What's Available" on page 16.

Flip Booklet Cover

Use with "Flip-The-Shapes Booklet" on page 16.

Flip the pages. Match each object on the bottom to its matching shape on the top.

Flip the shapes

©The Education Center, Inc. • *Shapes* • Preschool/Kindergarten • TEC3198

20

triangle

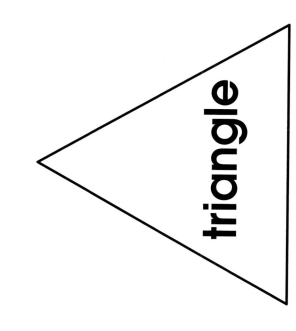

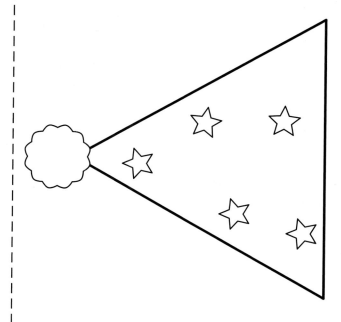

rectangle

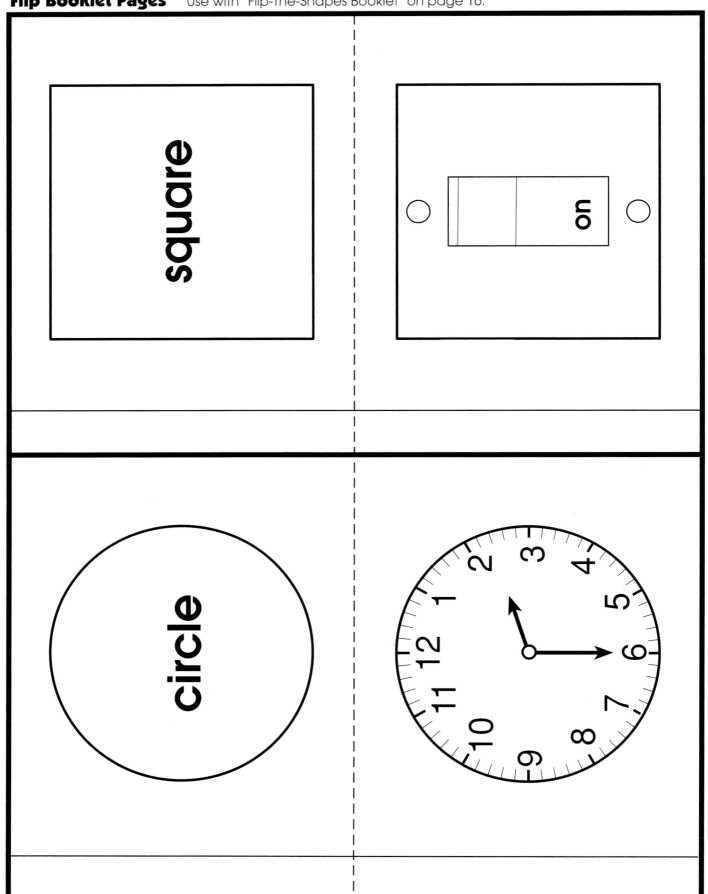

square

on

circle

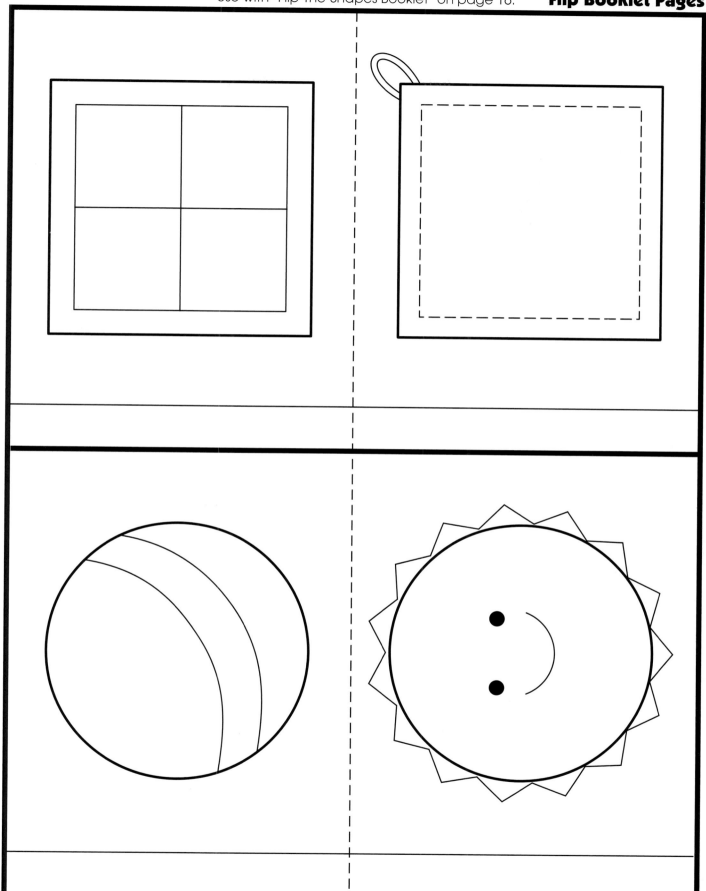

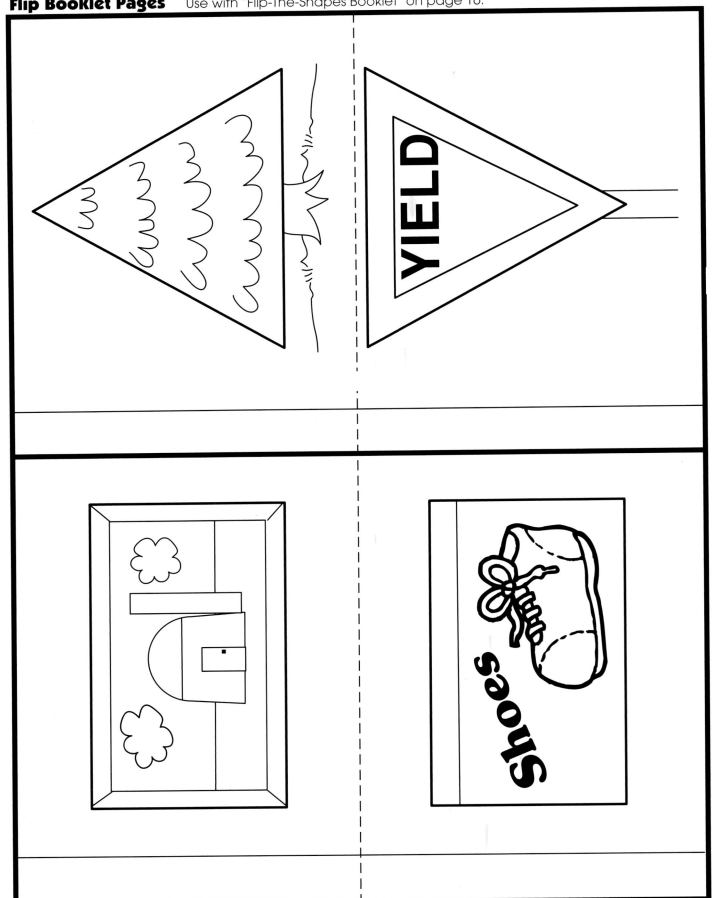

Circle Prints

How's this for shapely inspiration? In advance, fold eight paper towels and place each in a different sanitized meat tray. Saturate each of the paper towels in a different color of tempera paint. Locate objects which would make circular imprints, and place each on a paint-coated paper towel. To create the artwork, repeatedly press each object onto a large construction paper circle. On another day, trv the same technique featuring triangles, rectangles, or squares rather than circles.

Janet Paczak—Gr. K

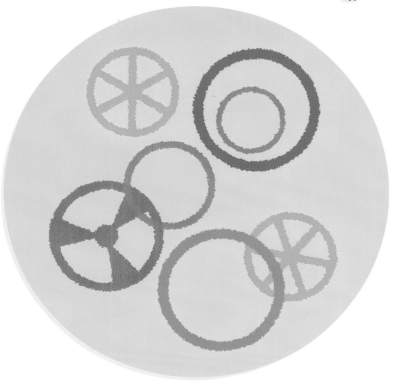

Let's Do The Twist

Come on, baby! Let's do the twist—the shapes twist, that is! In advance prepare a giant Twister® gameboard. Using a different color of construction paper for each different shape, cut out one 2" and two 5" circles, squares, triangles, ovals, rectangles, and diamonds. In random fashion, adhere the larger shapes to one side of a clear, vinyl tablecloth using clear Con-Tact® covering. To make a spinner, visually divide a tagboard circle into six sections; then glue one of the smaller shapes in each section. Laminate and attach a spinner. To play the game with a small group of children, place the gameboard on the floor with the smooth side facing upward. Ask each child in turn to spin the spinner and to identify the designated shape. Have him place either a foot or a hand on a matching shape on the gameboard. Continue play until each child has had several turns. Now your youngsters will really be in shape!

Karen Eiben—Pre-K
The Kid's Place, La Salle, IL

Painting Takes Shape

Little ones love to paint, and paint, and paint! With this idea, their creative efforts will really take shape. Using masking tape, tape the outlines of geometric shapes to large pieces of fingerpainting paper. Encourage a young artist to select a piece of paper and use brushes and paints to paint the entire sheet with the colors of her choice. When the paint is dry, assist the child as she carefully removes the tape. Surprise! What shapes did you paint?

Pat Johnson—Three-Year-Olds
Church of the Redeemer United Methodist Preschool
Columbus, OH

Come To Circle Time!

Your little ones will really get into shapes with this fun circle-time idea! As youngsters come to circle time, ask them to sit on the floor forming the shape they are currently learning about. For example, one week you might have your class sit in the shape of a triangle and another week you might have them sit in the shape of a square. This is not only a fun way to review shapes, but also a nifty way to conduct your circle-time activities!

Sandra Cothren
Lawrenceburg Child Development Center
Lawrenceburg, TN

Listen And Do

This activity tunes into children's listening and comprehension skills. To make a gameboard, glue two different colors of each of the four basic shapes onto a large piece of poster board. Add a decorative border to the poster board; then laminate it. On each of a supply of index cards, write directions telling a youngster to place a given number of counters on a particular color of shape. Decorate a small paper bag in which to store the direction cards and a supply of counters. To play, take the counters out of the bag; then have a child draw a card from the bag. Read the direction to the child and have him place the appropriate number of counters on the specified shape on the gameboard. Continue to play until there are counters on every shape on the gameboard.

Place 4 on the blue ●.

Place 8 on the red ■.

Mr. Blockhead

Sorting and classifying will be a cinch with Mr. Blockhead. In preparation, collect a box (such as a paper box) and several matching lids. Cover the box and lids with solid-colored Con-Tact® covering. On one side of the box, draw a simple face. On the top of each of the lids, trace the shapes of different shapes and sizes of blocks. Cut out these shapes using a utility knife. Place the box and the lids in your block area. To use them, a child puts a lid on the box and selects the blocks that correspond to the cut-out shapes. He then drops those blocks through the holes in the lid into the box. When the box is full, he removes the lid and dumps the blocks out to be sorted again.

Square Is In

Start at square one for this neat geometric art activity. Begin the project with one large construction paper square. Glue small squares atop the large one until it is nearly covered. Because this type of activity is a fun way to introduce shape units, try the same type of activity featuring triangles, rectangles, or circles rather than squares.

Pat Johnson—Three-Year-Olds
Church of the Redeemer United Methodist Preschool
Columbus, OH

Sunny-Day Shapes

A little fresh air and a few sticks of chalk can go a long way to reinforce shape recognition. On a nice sunny day, take your youngsters and a box or two of colored chalk to a surfaced section of your playground. Draw a large shape on the playground surface. Have children use chalk to trace that shape. Encourage youngsters to talk about the shape's characteristics as they work. Youngsters can also follow directions such as "Walk around the square," or "Jump inside the triangle." If your children are able, have them draw shapes independently. Then have each child move to a classmate's shape and trace that shape with another color of chalk.

Dawn Dumond—Grs. K-1
Mount View School, Thorndike, ME

Singing About Shapes

Before introducing this song, cut a supply of geometric shapes from construction paper. During a group time, provide each child with a shape. Then sing this song to the tune of "Mary Had A Little Lamb," substituting a different child's name with each verse. To prepare each child to respond successfully at the end of his verse, say, for example, "Let's sing our song to someone holding a triangle."

[Child's name] has a little shape,
Little shape, little shape.
[Child's name] has a little shape.
Please tell us what it is.

Carolyn Bryant—Pre-K
First Baptist Church Powder Springs
Powder Springs, GA

Musical Shapes

Come on, everybody! Step inside the circle, squeeze into the square, and round up into the rectangle! Your youngsters will enjoy this group activity that reinforces shape recognition and develops cooperation. To prepare, use colored tape to create large geometric-shaped outlines on the floor of an open area. (Make sure the outlines are big enough for a small group of children to stand inside.) Gather a group of youngsters in the area; then play a musical selection. Direct your little ones to hop, jump, walk, or otherwise move around the area. Stop the music; then name a shape. Encourage all of the children to gather inside the specified shape, helping each other by holding hands or by putting arms around each other. Your class will really be in shape now!

Janet S. Vaughn—Preschool Director
First Congregational Church Preschool
LaGrange, IL

A "Sense-sational" Quilt

Your youngsters won't want to take their hands off this textured quilt. In advance sew a fabric square for each child on a large piece of cloth. Provide each child with a variety of precut shapes of various textures such as sandpaper, cotton, foil, felt, satin, and corduroy. After discussing each texture and its characteristics with your class, have each child choose several shapes or textures of his choice. Have him glue his shapes onto a designated fabric square on the quilt. Hang the quilt at students' eye level. This is definitely a "Please Touch" kind of quilt!

Patricia Pereira—Three- And Four-Year-Olds
St. Stanislaus School
Fall River, MA

Edible Triangles

To review shape recognition and stir up some good eating, try this nifty cooking activity. Cut a piece of pita bread in half. Cut the halves into small triangle shapes Brush the top of each triangle with softened butter. Spread one tablespoon of pizza sauce on the top. Sprinkle it with shredded mozzarella and bake until the cheese melts. Your youngsters will love this yummy triangular treat.

Kim Ennis—Gr. K, Smiths Primary, Smiths, AL

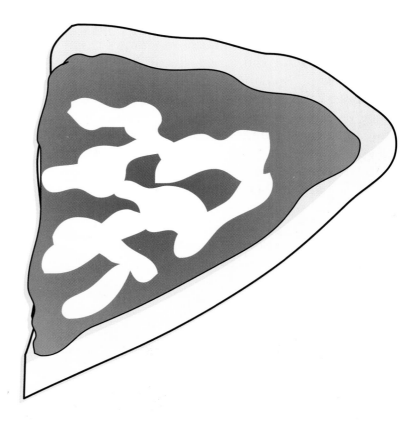

Giant Shape Dominoes

In this game of giant, shape dominoes, students string shapes together to cover the classroom floor! Use 9" x 12" sheets of black construction paper to make a large set of dominoes. Cut out basic shapes from sponges. Use flourescent paint and sponge-paint two shapes on each black sheet, as shown. Laminate shape dominoes. Place one domino on the floor. Deal out the other dominoes. In turn, students try to put a matching shape adjacent to one on the floor. Continue until all dominoes have been paired with their appropriate shapes.

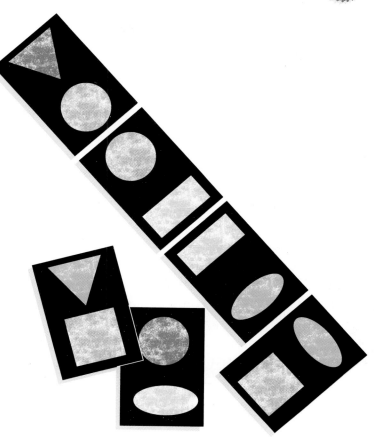

Shapes With Charisma

Pipe cleaners aside, no one will get bent out of shape over this art activity. Tape four pipe cleaners to a poster board shape for arms and legs. For feet and hands, tape small versions of the same shape to the unattached ends of the pipe cleaners. Add wiggle eyes or pom-pom eyes, before drawing other facial features with a black marker. Attach tufts of fake fur, crumpled tissue-paper strips, or curling ribbon for hair, if desired. Bend the pipe cleaners to pose your irresistible shape creature.

Tammy Woodel
Duson Elementary
Duson, LA

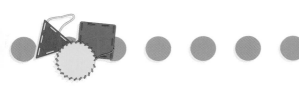

Spinning Circles

Exploring circles in your classroom? Give this creative idea a spin. For each child, cut a construction-paper circle to match the size of your record player's turntable. Have a child press her circle onto the turntable. Turn on the record player and direct the child to hold the tip of a marker as still as possible on the paper. As the turntable spins, circles will appear. For added fun, encourage the child to change marker colors. The sounds from all of this circle excitement will be music to your ears!

Cindi Zsittnik—Pre-K
Surrey Child Care Center
Hagerstown, MD

Copycat

To reinforce shape recognition, play a game of Copycat with a youngster at your sand table. Make sure that the sand is damp; then use an unsharpened pencil to draw a geometric shape in the sand. Provide the child with a pencil and encourage him to copy the shape in the sand. As a challenge, have the child carefully observe as you draw a shape; then wipe the shape away. Encourage him to draw the same shape in the sand.

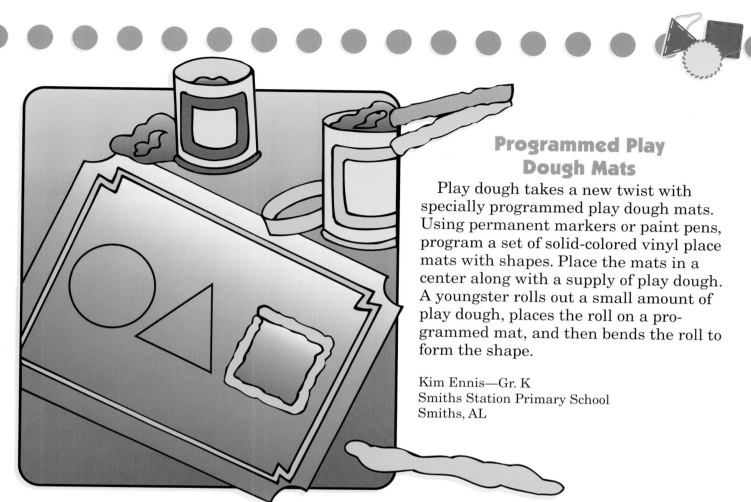

Programmed Play Dough Mats

Play dough takes a new twist with specially programmed play dough mats. Using permanent markers or paint pens, program a set of solid-colored vinyl place mats with shapes. Place the mats in a center along with a supply of play dough. A youngster rolls out a small amount of play dough, places the roll on a programmed mat, and then bends the roll to form the shape.

Kim Ennis—Gr. K
Smiths Station Primary School
Smiths, AL

Chinese Jump Rope Shapes

Here's a shape recognition activity that youngsters will be anxious to jump into with both feet! Challenge pairs or small groups of youngsters to simulate simple shapes by positioning themselves in strategic points and stretching a Chinese jump rope around their ankles. If a Chinese jump rope is not available, you can make your own by stitching the ends of a long piece of elastic to form a circle. This "feet-on" approach is sure to make shape recognition a snap for your youngsters.

Joyce Montag
Slippery Rock, PA

Musical Shape Book

Sing yourself into shapes. For each child, you will need six pages of white construction paper and a cover. Duplicate each of the first six lines of "The Shape Song" onto a separate page of the book. Have each child illustrate her pages and cover before stapling the pages together in order with the cover. Sing "The Shape Song" by beginning with the text on page one. At the end of page six, go back to page one and continue singing through page three. When you have mastered English, try Spanish!

The Shape Song
(sung to the tune of "Twinkle, Twinkle")

Rectangle, circle, *(page one)*
Triangle, square. *(page two)*
I can be found anywhere! *(page three)*
On a hat *(page four)*
On a house *(page five)*
Even on a little mouse. *(page six)*
Rectangle, circle,
Triangle, square.
I can be found anywhere!

Rectángulo, círculo,
Triángulo, cuadrado.
¡Me pueden encontrar por todo lado!
En un sombrerito
En una casa
También en un ratón loquito.
Rectángulo, círculo,
Triángulo, cuadrado.
¡Me pueden encontrar por todo lado!

Evie Guerrat—Gr. K, Ulatis Elementary, Vacaville, CA

Shape Party

Munch your way through shapes with a shape party. Assign each child a shape and ask him to bring in a food in that shape. For example, if the shape is a circle, a child could bring in banana slices, cookies, carrot coins, or M&M's®.

Shari O'Shea—Gr. K
Conewago Elementary School
Elizabethtown, PA

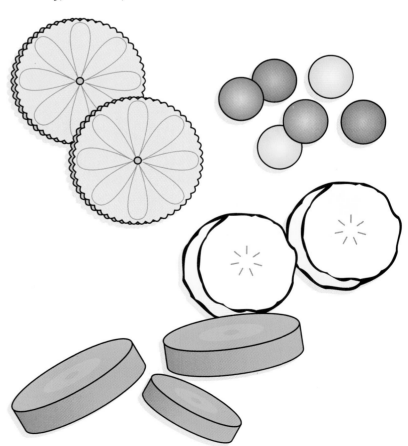

Lacing Shapes

Give students additional fine-motor practice with these inexpensive lacing shapes. To make the lacing shapes, cut shapes from solid-colored plastic placemats. Using a hole puncher, punch holes around the perimeter of each shape. Place the shapes in a center along with a supply of brightly colored laces.

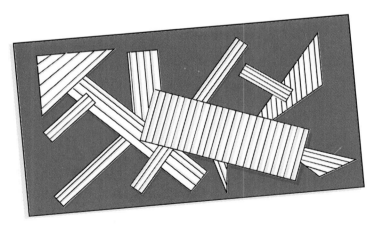

Lightbulb-Carton Collage

Have youngsters explore a new texture when you provide the liners from lightbulb cartons for collages. Encourage students to cut the liners into different sizes and shapes and to glue them onto paper to create interesting designs.

Mary E. Maurer
Caddo, OK

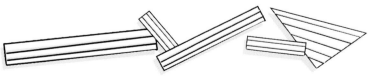

In Shape With Shapes

When it's time to get into shapes, try this activity. As each shape is studied, prepare a large cutout and a collection of small cutouts of the same shape for each child. Have each child glue as many of the small shapes onto her larger shape as desired. Count and record the number of smaller shapes with the child. Shape recognition is sure to stick!

Cindy Crosby
Summerville Baptist Preschool
Summerville, SC

Musical Shapes

Listen to the beat; then take a seat with this fun game. In advance, prepare two identical sets of construction-paper shapes. Each set must be equal in number to your class enrollment. Keep one of the sets for yourself, and from the other set, give one shape to each child. Arrange the children's chairs in musical-chairs fashion. To play, have children march in a wide circle around the chairs as music plays. While the children march, place a shape from your set of shapes on each of the chairs. Whenever you like, stop the music and each child scatters to be seated in a chair displaying a shape that matches his shape. As children's abilities permit, redistribute the shapes and play again.

Sort Of Hungry? Eat Your Shapes!

You'll be delighted to watch students sort, count, and make patterns with these "math-licious" crackers! In advance, purchase a variety of different-shaped crackers. To use, encourage youngsters to empty the crackers into a bowl. Have them sort the crackers by shape. Assist them in making simple patterns with the crackers. Count the crackers as they are dropped back into the appropriate boxes. Allow time for shapely snacking!

Shape Bears

These furry friends make shape discrimination easier to bear. Glue a set of shape cutouts to the overalls of each of several large bear cutouts. Attach a Press-On Pocket (available from The Education Center, Inc.) to the bib of each bear's overalls. Cut an assortment of matching shapes from construction paper and hide them around the classroom. In turn, each youngster finds a shape, identifies it, and places it in the matching bear's pocket. Shape-recognition skills will take shape in no time!

Andrea Hartman—Preschool Handicapped
Martinsburg, WV

Shapes Galore

Use this activity to enhance shape recognition and creativity. In advance, cut a supply of shapes in a variety of sizes and colors. Provide a selection of different-colored construction paper for youngsters to use as backgrounds. Have each child create a picture or design by gluing shapes onto a background. Things are beginning to take shape around here!

Lisa Anne Totora—Pre-K
First United Methodist Church
New Orleans, LA

Shapes Activity

Here's a sweet way to reinforce shape recognition while promoting creativity. Provide youngsters with miniature marshmallows, toothpicks, and a dark piece of construction paper. Have each child use the marshmallows and tooth-picks to make triangles, rectangles, and squares. Then encourage each child to create his own design using toothpicks and marshmallows. Glue the design onto the construction paper. These wonderful works of art make a great display in any classroom.

B. L. Scholtz—Gr. K
St. Ann's School
Charlotte, NC

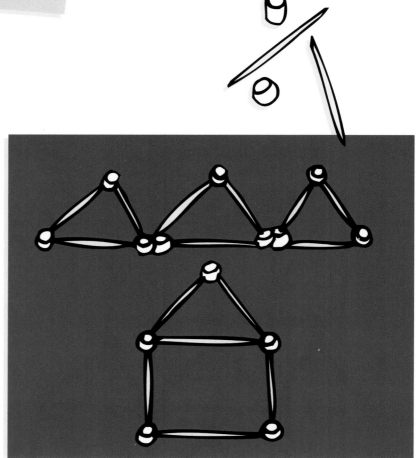

Reproducible Activities...

The Little Engine That Could™

Materials Needed

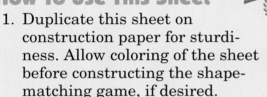

— scissors
— two brads per child
— hole punch

How To Use This Sheet

1. Duplicate this sheet on construction paper for sturdiness. Allow coloring of the sheet before constructing the shape-matching game, if desired.
2. For construction ease, this sheet is designed to be cut across on the bold horizontal line only. The outline of the train does not need to be cut out. Cut out the indentation on each train wheel.
3. Cut out each shape circle.
4. Punch the center hole of each circle and each train wheel with a hole punch.
5. Place the shape wheels behind the train and attach each wheel with a brad.
6. Turn the shape wheels until matching shapes show in the indentations in the train wheels.
7. Send the train home for continued practice. The directions are on the game for parents to read and play along.

Finished Sample

Turn the wheels.
Match the shapes.

Shape Train

Matthew
name

Turn the wheels.
Match the shapes.

Shape Train

name

©The Education Center, Inc. • *Shapes*
• Preschool/Kindergarten • TEC3198

How To Use This Sheet

1. Duplicate the sheet on construction paper for sturdiness.
2. Cut the gameboard and playing pieces apart by cutting on the dotted lines.
3. The children sort the game pieces by matching the shape embedded in each piece's illustration to the basic shape outline on the gameboard.
4. Send the game home in a Ziploc® bag with the parent note below for continued practice.

Parent Note

Dear Parent,

Hop aboard the shape train! We have been learning our shapes at school and learning that shapes are all around us. To play this game, turn the small playing pieces facedown on a table. Place the shape train gameboard faceup. Allow your child to turn over a playing card and name the shape. Have your child place the card on the corresponding shape car on the train gameboard.

For an extra challenge, as your child turns up each card, ask him to find something in the room that is the same shape. Helping your child recognize familiar shapes in his surroundings is an essential prereading skill. For even more fun, the next time you go to the library, look for books about trains or shapes!

All aboard for shape fun!

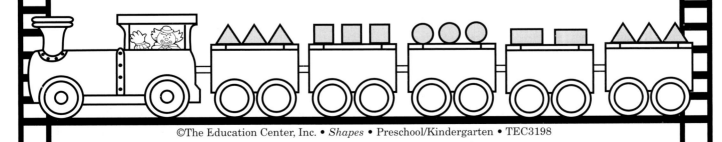

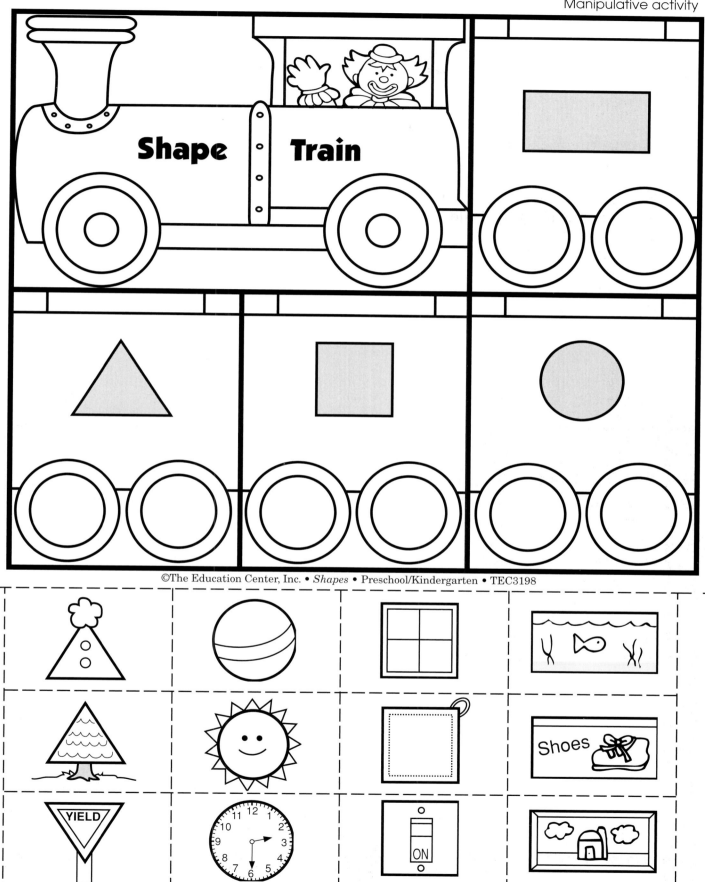

Shape **Train**

©The Education Center, Inc. • *Shapes* • Preschool/Kindergarten • TEC3198

Shapely Snakes

Patterns

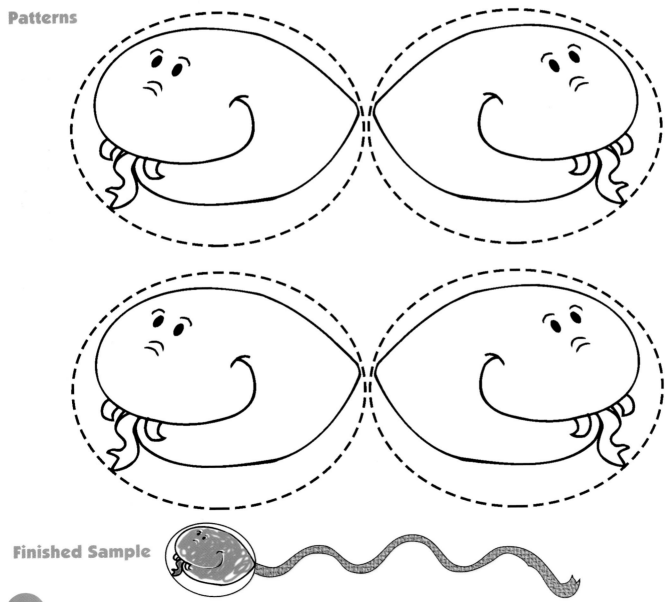

Finished Sample

Name _____

Slither In A Circle

Trace.

Color the ◯ s.

45

Shapely Snake's Squares

Name

Trace.

Color the ☐ s.

46

Shapely Strikes Again

Name

Trace.

Color the △s.

Name _____

Rectangle Reptile

Trace.

Color the ▭ s.

©The Education Center, Inc. • *Shapes* • Preschool/Kindergarten • TEC3198